OTHER HELEN EXLEY GIFTBOOKS IN THIS SERIES:
A Century of Cricket Jokes     A Round of Golf Jokes
A Binge of Diet Jokes     A Bouquet of Wedding Jokes

Published simultaneously in 1998 by Exley Publications Ltd in Great
Britain, and Exley Publications LLC in the USA.

24  23  22  21  20  19  18  17  16  15  14  13

Cartoons © Bill Stott 1998
Copyright © Helen Exley 1998
The moral right of the author has been asserted.
**ISBN 1-86187-020-5**
A copy of the CIP data is available from the British Library on request.
**Series Editor: Helen Exley**
**Editor: Claire Lipscomb**
Printed and bound in China.

**Exley Publications Ltd, 16 Chalk Hill, Watford, Herts WD19 4BG, UK.**
**Exley Publications LLC, 185 Main Street, Spencer, MA 01562, USA.**
**www.helenexleygiftbooks.com**

Acknowledgements: The publishers are grateful for permission to reproduce copyright
material. Whilst every reasonable effort has been made to trace copyright holders, the
publishers would be pleased to hear from any not here acknowledged. BILL COSBY: From *Time
Flies* published by Bantam Books. © 1987 William H. Cosby Jr. Reprinted by permission
Doubleday, a division of Bantam Doubleday Dell Publishing Group. EDWARD ENFIELD: From
*The Oldie, The World According to Enfield Senior,* © 1997 Edward Enfield. Published by Oldie
Publications Ltd. KEVIN GOLDSTEIN-JACKSON: From *Joke... After Joke... After Joke.* Reprinted
by permission of Elliot Right Way Books. CHRISTOPHER MATTHEW: From *How to Survive
Middle Age,* © 1982 Christopher Matthew, published by Hodder and Stoughton. Reprinted by
permission of Rogers, Coleridge and White. MARY McBRIDE: From *Grandma Knows Best, But
No One Ever Listens!* published by Meadowbrook Press, Minnetonka, © 1987 Mary McBride.
OGDEN NASH: "Crossing The Boarder" from *Marriage Lines* © 1956 Ogden Nash, renewed
1984 by Frances Nash, Isabel Nash Eberstadt, Linnell Nash Smith. Reprinted by permission of
Curtis Brown Ltd, Andre Deutsch and Little, Brown and Co.

# A JUBILEE OF
# OVER 60s'
# JOKES

## CARTOONS BY
## BILL STOTT

**EXLEY**

*"SIXTY! WHEN I WAS NINE I THOUGHT TWELVE WAS <u>OLD</u>!"*

## When Does "Old" Begin?

"Old age is when you can't quite decide whether you've saved too little or stayed too long."
ROBERT ORBEN, from *2100 Laughs for All Occasions*

\*

"Age. That period of life in which we compound for the vices that remain by reviling those we have no longer the vigor to commit."

AMBROSE BIERCE

"I do not call myself really old yet. Not till a young woman offers me her seat in a railway compartment will that tragedy really be mine."

E.V. LUCAS

Senescence begins
And middle age ends
The day your descendents
Outnumber your friends.

OGDEN NASH, from *Crossing the Boarder*

*

*"WOW! THE 1930s! WERE THERE DINOSAURS THEN, GRAN?"*

<u>PREHISTORIC!</u>

"When I was young, the Dead Sea was still alive."
GEORGE BURNS

\*

"Old? She is approaching middle age for the third time."

"Old? His toupee turned gray."
LEOPOLD FECHTNER

\*

"Her birthday cake had so many candles on it she was fined for air pollution."
E.C. MCKENZIE, from *14,000 Quips and Quotes for Writers and Speakers*

\*

"You know you're ancient when you can remember a time when errors were blamed on human beings rather than computers."
NICOLE REUBEN

\*

*"DID YOU EVER MEET ANY ROMANS, GRANDAD?"*

## THOSE TELLTALE SIGNS...

"There are three ways to tell if you're getting on: people of your own age start looking older than you; you become convinced you're suddenly equipped with a snooze button; and you start getting symptoms in the places you used to get urges."

DENIS NORDEN

\*

"You know you're getting old when you stoop to tie your shoes and wonder what else you can do while you're down there."

GEORGE BURNS

\*

"You know you're getting older when you order stewed prunes and the waiter says 'excellent choice.'"

from *Old Age is not for Sissies*

\*

"... there are three signs of aging.
The first is that you tend to forget things rather
easily – and for the life of me, I don't know
what the other two things are."

EMANUEL CELLER

*"DON'T WORRY ABOUT IT – YOU DON'T LOOK A DAY OVER 50.*

*MIND YOU, YOU ALWAYS WERE A MATURE 50...."*

*" COURSE I'M OLDER THAN MY HUSBAND...."*

## Putting A Brave Face On It

"Two fraternity brothers were attending their class reunion, the first time they'd seen one another for thirty years. One asked, 'Is your wife still as pretty as she was when we were all in school together?'

'Yeah, she is... but it takes her an hour longer.'"

from *A Treasury of Senior Humor*

\*

"When you reach sixty your beautician sends you this letter. It says, 'Dear Customer, I can no longer help you. From this day on you're on your own.'"

MICHELE KOLFF

\*

"As a woman grows older, she starts to suspect that nature is plotting against her for the benefit of doctors, dentists, and moisturizer magnates."

NICOLE REUBENS

\*

"YOU KNOW YOU'RE OVER THE HILL WHEN YOUR MOST-LOVED

FILMS ARE SHOWN AT 11 O'CLOCK IN THE MORNING...."

## YOU KNOW YOU'RE OVER 60...

"... when you really think that you can predict the weather by the feeling in your shin bones."

"... when you start receiving birthday cards which don't mention your age."

"... when you start wearing silly hats."

"... when you think *Baywatch* is a real documentary, and feel concerned that the lifeguards aren't wearing overcoats."

"... when you think a C.D. is a medical condition."

"... when you don't bother buying an answerphone because you're always in."

JON NEWBOLD

✳

## A Sensitive Subject

"I am just turning forty and taking
my time about it."

HAROLD LLOYD, at 77, when asked his age, from *The Times*

\*

"I don't need you to remind me of my age, I have
a bladder to do that for me."

STEPHEN FRY, from *Paperweight*

"YES HE IS GOOD – JUST DON'T ASK HIM HOW OLD HE IS...."

## A Maintenance Problem

"Old? Listen, when you get past sixty you're a maintenance problem."

CALEY O'ROURKE

\*

"People think of growing old like a disease you catch when you get to about sixty."

EAMONN BRENNAN, age 13, from *Happy Birthday You Poor Old Wreck*

\*

"Old age is when most of the names in your little black book are doctors."

E.C. MCKENZIE, from *14,000 Quips and Quotes for Writers and Speakers*

\*

"You know you're getting on when your bottom hits the settee before you've even sat down, and the supermarket trolley rattles less than your dentures."

JON NEWBOLD

\*

"After a certain age, if you don't wake up aching in every joint, you are probably dead."

TOMMY MEIN

*"WHY DON'T WE HAVE A BATH TOGETHER, LIKE WE USED TO? I*
*DON'T MIND HELPING YOU IN AND OUT...."*

*"YOU KNOW WHAT THEY SAY ABOUT PETS GROWING TO LOOK*
*LIKE THEIR OWNERS?"*

## The Good Old Days

"That sign of old age, extolling the past at the
expense of the present."

SYDNEY SMITH

*

"Being disillusioned with the modern world is our
favorite hobby – no, it's our responsibility."

NIELA ELIASON, from Kitchen Tables and Other Midlife Musings

"It's hard for me to get used to these changing times. I can remember when the air was clean and sex was dirty."

GEORGE BURNS

*

"We tend to forget one of the reasons why they were called 'the good old days'. The days were old but we weren't."

ROBERT ORBEN, from 2100 Laughs for All Occasions

*

*"I THINK YOU SUIT BEING 60. YOU'VE ALWAYS HAD AN OLD FACE...."*

"GRANDMA BEAT HIM AT HIS OWN VIDEO GAME AGAIN...."

"For every baby born, two women turn into grandmas. As a new grandma, you will look in the mirror and think, 'I'm too young to be a grandma.' But you have to face reality. You are old enough to be a grandma if...

When you raise your arm to wave, the flab underneath waves first.

You decide to find a job and discover the references on your last résumé are all deceased.

The aerobics instructor looks at you when she says, 'Everybody take a rest.'

The things you want to talk about when you see your doctor take more than one sheet of paper.

You don't care what the dentist says about your teeth, as long as he says you can keep them."

MARY MCBRIDE, from *Grandma Knows Best, But No One Ever Listens!*

\*

*"NOTWITHSTANDING ANYTHING I SAID ON OUR WEDDING*
*NIGHT... I'VE GOT CRAMP!"*

"Young men want to be faithful and are not, old men want to be faithless and cannot."

OSCAR WILDE

\*

"Sex after ninety is like trying to shoot pool with a rope. Even putting my cigar in its holder is a thrill."

GEORGE BURNS

\*

"Lola's husband Joseph, a merchant, was asked why he subscribed to *Playboy* magazine. 'I read *Playboy* for the same reason that I read *National Geographic,* so's I can see all the sights I'm too danged old to visit.'"

from A Treasury of Senior Humor

*

"Sex after sixty: When relighting your fire means paying the overdue gas bill."

JON NEWBOLD

*

"At my age, by the time I find temptation, I'm too tired to give in to it."

E.C. MCKENZIE, from *14,000 Quips and Quotes for Writers and Speakers*

*

"The dead bird does not leave the nest."

WINSTON CHURCHILL, on being advised that his fly was open

*

*"I WONDER WHAT YOU'D LOOK LIKE WITHOUT YOUR CHINS...."*

*"HMMM."*

"*Face Lift:* The classic beauty operation whereby the surgeon makes an incision under cover of the hairline, pulls the facial skin taut, puts in a tuck and cuts off the remains. If performed too many times, a patient could end up with his tummy button up his nose.

*Blepharoplasty:* The operation that takes away the bags under your eyes, the better to allow them to open in stunned disbelief at the subsequent bill.

*Chemical Peel:* ... a hair- (not to say skin-) raising method of burning the wrinkles off the face with strong chemicals, or possibly with a rotating wire brush. For those who fancy a complexion like a brick wall."

CHRISTOPHER MATTHEW, from *How to Survive Middle Age*

\*

"How foolish to think that one can ever slam the door in the face of age. Much wiser to be polite and gracious and ask him to lunch in advance."

NOËL COWARD

\*

"YES, YES, A GOOD BODY FOR A MAN OF 60, BUT YOU'RE ONLY HERE TO HAVE YOUR BUNIONS TREATED...."

*"OH NO! ANOTHER IMAGE REVAMP."*

"When you've reached a certain age and think
that a face-lift or a trendy way of dressing will make
you feel twenty years younger, remember – nothing
can fool a flight of stairs."

DENIS NORDEN

∗

"When you're my age, you go out to the beach
and turn a wonderful color. Blue. It's from holding
in your stomach."

ROBERT ORBEN, from *2100 Laughs for All Occasions*

∗

"YOU DANCE JUST LIKE YOU DID 30 YEARS AGO – BADLY!"

## When "Bop Till You Drop" Takes On A Sinister Meaning

"One of the first signs of getting old is when your head makes dates your body can't keep."

KEVIN GOLDSTEIN-JACKSON,
from *Joke... After Joke... After Joke...*

\*

"Old age is when it takes you longer to get over a good time than to have it."

E.C. MCKENZIE,
from *14,000 Quips and Quotes for Writers and Speakers*

\*

"I'm at an age where my back goes out more than I do."

PHYLLIS DILLER

\*

*"ACTUALLY, I'M 60 BUT MY HAIR'S ONLY 2."*

## Baldness: The Fringe Benefits

1. There is never any hassle with dress codes, flaky dandruff or trying to get that full-bodied look.

2. You save countless hours and dollars at hair salons.

3. You can use your head as a reflector when lost at sea.

DAVID E. BESWICK, from *Bald Men Always Come Out On Top*

\*

*"I DO WISH YOU WOULDN'T DO THAT...."*

*"THEY WOULDN'T SERVE ME – SAID I DIDN'T LOOK OLD ENOUGH. YOU'LL HAVE TO GO."*

"It is possible that a man could live twice as long if he didn't spend the first half of his life acquiring habits that shorten the other half."
E.C. MCKENZIE, from *14,000 Quips and Quotes for Writers and Speakers*

*

"A woman walked up to a little old man rocking in a chair on his porch. 'I couldn't help noticing how happy you look,' she said. 'What's your secret for a long, happy life?'

'I smoke three packs of cigarettes a day,' he said. 'I also drink a case of whiskey a week, eat fatty foods, and never exercise.'

'That's amazing,' the woman said. 'How old are you?'

'Twenty-six,' he said."
JOE CLARO, from *The Random House Book of Jokes and Anecdotes*

*

"The secret of staying young is to live honestly, eat slowly, and lie about your age."
LUCILLE BALL

*

## SPARE PARTS!

"Many people... do not want all the confusion that trifocals bring and prefer instead to go through life using three different pairs of glasses: one pair for reading, one pair for middle distance, and one pair for lunar eclipses."

BILL COSBY, from *Time Flies*

\*

"I know a fella who had one of those hair transplants and it was kind of touching. He bought a comb and asked if it came with instructions!"

ROBERT ORBEN, from *2100 Laughs for All Occasions*

\*

"You have arrived at old age when all you can put your teeth into is a glass."

E.C. MCKENZIE, from *14,000 Quips and Quotes for Writers and Speakers*

## RULES FOR RETIREMENT

● Do not follow your wife around the house when she is hoovering. This is not only irritating, it is positively dangerous. A friend of mine broke his Achilles tendon by tripping over the hoover flex.

● Take a calcium pill every day. I got this from a friend who went on a pre-retirement course costing [thousands], paid for by somebody else. "What have you learned?" I asked when he came back.

"I have learned that everyone over sixty should take a calcium pill every day."

"Anything else?"

"No."

Bearing in mind the cost of the course, in passing on this nugget to *Oldie* readers I reckon that for once at least this column is giving value for money.

EDWARD ENFIELD, from "New Tricks for Old Dogs", in *The Oldie*, *The World According to Enfield Senior*

\*

"WHEN I SUGGESTED A HOBBY AFTER WE RETIRED, I WAS

THINKING OF GARDENING...."

## One Day At A Time...

"... at my time of life to look to the future is to take a very short-term view of things."

EDWARD ENFIELD,
from *The Oldie, The World According to Enfield Senior*

"A young real estate agent was pushing hard to sell an apartment to this old codger. After praising its numerous attractions, he ended his hard-sell with, 'Remember, Mr. Brown, this is an investment for the future.'

'Listen, young man,' said Mr. Brown wearily, 'at my time of life I don't even buy green bananas.'"

JENNY DE SOUZA

*

"My neighbor has arrived at the age where, if he drops $10 in the collection plate, it's not a contribution – it's an investment."

ROBERT ORBEN, from *2100 Laughs for All Occasions*

## RESPECT YOUR ELDERS

"The best part of being an oldie is that you get to be eccentric and young people have to be polite and patronize your idiosyncrasies."
NIELA ELIASON, from *Kitchen Tables and Other Midlife Musings*

\*

"From the earliest times the old have rubbed it into the young that they are wiser than they, and before the young had discovered what nonsense this was they were old too, and it profited them to carry on the imposture."
WILLIAM SOMERSET MAUGHAM,
from *Cakes and Ale*

\*

"I was brought up to respect my elders and now I don't have to respect *anybody*."
GEORGE BURNS, at 87

\*

*"HE BET HIS ALLOWANCE THAT HE COULD DO MORE
PRESS-UPS THAN GRANDAD. HE LOST."*

*"I don't feel old, just downright worn out."*

WILL SMITH, age 110

\*

"Age seldom arrives smoothly or quickly. It's more often a succession of jerks."

JEAN RHYS

\*

"Old? He gets tired brushing his teeth."

LEOPOLD FECHTNER

\*

"You're getting old when almost everything hurts, and what doesn't hurt doesn't work."

E.C. MCKENZIE,
from *14,000 Quips and Quotes for Writers and Speakers*

\*

"I smoke cigars because at my age if I don't have something to hang onto I might fall down."

GEORGE BURNS

\*

"YOU KNOW WHAT THEY SAY ABOUT BEING AS OLD AS YOU
FEEL? I THINK I'M ABOUT 328."

60

"The couple had just reached retirement age, but Mr. Robinson was a very worried man.

'We don't really have enough to live on,' he confessed to his wife. 'Sure, our pension is enough to survive – but we lack sufficient savings to give us a few extra pleasures like the occasional evening at the cinema or a decent holiday once a year.'

'Don't worry,' replied Mrs. Robinson. 'I've managed to save a few thousand pounds.'

'However did you manage that?'

'Well,' said Mrs. Robinson, a bit shyly, 'every time you made love to me these past thirty years I've put fifty pence in my own bank account.'

'But why did you keep it a secret all these years?' demanded Mr. Robinson. 'If I'd known about it I'd have given you all my business.'"

KEVIN GOLDSTEIN-JACKSON, from *Joke... After Joke... After Joke...*

\*

"Although I just can't take the plunge into bean sprouts or alfalfa, one day I did put a few carrot sticks and celery stalks into a bag and I took a healthful walk in the park. After a while, I sat down on a bench beside an old man, who was both smoking and eating a chocolate bar, two serious violations of a longevity diet.

'Do you mind my asking how old you are?' I said.

'Ninety-two,' he replied.

'Well, if you smoke and eat *that* stuff, you're gonna die.'

He took a hard look at my carrots and celery, and then he said, '*You're* dead *already*.'"

BILL COSBY, from Time Flies

*

"Longevity is one of the more dubious rewards of virtue."

NGAIO MARSH

*

"Aging seems to be the only available way to live a long time."

DANIEL-FRANÇOIS-ESPRIT AUBER

*

"OH JOY! OUR MEDICAL INSURANCE SAYS I'M QUALIFIED TO APPLY FOR A HEAD TRANSPLANT IN THREE YEARS' TIME!"

# "Exercise daily.
## Eat wisely.
### Die anyway."

AUTHOR UNKNOWN

## GROWING OLD DISGRACEFULLY

"Sex got me into trouble from the age of fifteen:
I'm hoping that by the time I'm seventy I'll
straighten it out."

HAROLD ROBBINS

*

*"SO YOU'RE 60. SO WHAT? A BIRTHDAY'S A BIRTHDAY!"*

"Old age doesn't stop men from chasing women – it's just they can't remember why."

JENNY DE SOUZA

\*

"The only thing I regret about my past life is the length of it. If I had my past life over again I'd make all the same mistakes – only sooner."

TALLULAH BANKHEAD,
quoted in *The Times*, July 28, 1981

\*

"One should never make one's debut with a scandal. One should reserve that to give an interest to one's old age."

OSCAR WILDE

\*

## A PHYSICAL WRECK

"A couple in their sixties are on their second honeymoon, reminiscing about the good old days when they were newlyweds. Full of nostalgia, the wife says, 'Do you recall how you used to nibble on my ear lobes?'

'Yes,' replies her husband.

'Well, why don't you do it anymore?'

'Because by the time I've put my teeth in, the urge has gone!'"

JENNY DE SOUZA

*

"Actually sixty isn't such a bad old age. All right, my eyesight's getting a bit weak, and my teeth keep falling out every time I brush them. But have you seen the price of false ones? No thanks! There are lots of exciting things that you can do with semolina.... My attention span – that's down to three minutes and falling. But there's one good thing – at least I've got my health...."

MIKE KNOWLES

*"DON'T WORRY ABOUT IT – IT HAPPENS QUITE OFTEN ON OUR*

*SECOND HONEYMOON BREAKS...."*

"60? AMAZING, THAT'S WONDERFUL – I HAD YOU AT LEAST 70 –
WE WERE AT THE SAME SCHOOL – REMEMBER?"

## SOME ADVANTAGES OF BEING OVER 60...

It's not all doom and gloom. Along with the wrinkles, hair-loss and clicking knees, your sixtieth birthday does bring some undeniable advantages:

1. You can cunningly pretend not to hear anything you don't want to hear.

2. You can enjoy the cheek of telling the grandchildren not to do what you did.

3. Your extra chin can act as a book rest.

JON NEWBOLD

\*

"Being sixty brings out certain advantages. For example, from now on your birthday cake is going to get bigger and bigger as they try to fit all those candles on."

MIKE KNOWLES

\*

"One of the nice things about old age is that you can whistle while you brush your teeth."

E.C. MCKENZIE, from *14,000 Quips and Quotes for Writers and Speakers*

\*

# "It's funny how we never get too old to learn some new ways to be foolish."

E.C. MCKENZIE, from *14,000 Quips and Quotes for Writers and Speakers*

*"THERE'S NO WAY HE WOULD HAVE DONE THAT AT YOUR AGE SON...."*

*"REPEAT AFTER ME... 'I'M 60, BUT I'M NOT AN OLD WRECK....'"*

## TOO YOUNG TO BE OLD

"Retirement at sixty-five is ridiculous. When I was sixty-five I still had pimples."

GEORGE BURNS

✳

"Growing old is more like a bad habit which a busy man has no time to form."

ANDRÉ MAUROIS

"The day I give in and allow the word bifocal to enter my vocabulary, is the day I'll also stop dying my roots, having my teeth capped and cantilevering my boobs. It'll be a courageous moment and fortunately I shall be too dead to see it. 'Glasses to glasses and bust to bust...'"

MAUREEN LIPMAN, from *You Can Read Me Like A Book*

*

*"NOW, THAT'S WHAT A GRANDMA SHOULD LOOK LIKE, GRANDMA."*